An Animal Family

LIONS AND CUBS

By Natalie Humphrey

Gareth Stevens
PUBLISHING

Please visit our website, www.garethstevens.com. For a free color catalog of all our high-quality books, call toll free 1-800-542-2595 or fax 1-877-542-2596.

Library of Congress Cataloging-in-Publication Data

Names: Humphrey, Natalie, author.
Title: Lions and cubs / Natalie Humphrey.
Description: New York : Gareth Stevens Publishing, 2021. | Series: An animal family | Includes index.
Identifiers: LCCN 2019045313 | ISBN 9781538255803 (library binding) | ISBN 9781538255780 (paperback) | ISBN 9781538255797 (6 Pack)| ISBN 9781538255810 (ebook)
Subjects: LCSH: Lion–Infancy–Juvenile literature. | Lion–Development–Juvenile literature.
Classification: LCC QL737.C23 H858 2021 | DDC 599.75713/92–dc23
LC record available at https://lccn.loc.gov/2019045313

First Edition

Published in 2021 by
Gareth Stevens Publishing
111 East 14th Street, Suite 349
New York, NY 10003

Editor: Natalie Humphrey
Designer: Katelyn E. Reynolds

Photo credits: Cover, p. 1 Rudi Hulshof/Shutterstock.com; pp. 5, 24 (pride) oNabby/Shutterstock.com; pp. 7, 23, 24 (cub) Sue Green/Shutterstock.com; p. 9 Keith Jenkinson/Shutterstock.com; p. 11 Dave Pusey/Shutterstock.com; p. 13 Frederic Coubet/Gallo Images/Getty Images Plus; p. 15 Nimit Virdi/500px/Getty Images; p. 17 Picture by Tambako the Jaguar/Moment/Getty Images; p. 19 santanu nandy/Moment/Getty Images; p. 21 Michele Burgess/Photolibrary/Getty Images Plus.

Printed in the United States of America

CPSIA compliance information: Batch #CS20GS: For further information contact Gareth Stevens, New York, New York at 1-800-542-2595.

Contents

Lions live in prides.
They are big families.

A cub is a baby lion.

Cubs are born every two years.

Mothers have two
at a time.
Some have four!

The pride looks after the cubs.

Cubs drink milk.
Their mothers make it.

Then they eat meat.

Cubs learn to hunt.
Mothers teach them.

Lions sleep 18 to 20 hours a day.

They hunt at night.

Words to Know

cub

pride

Index